HOW TO REMEMBER EVERYTHING

Professor Richard Wiseman is based at the University of Hertfordshire, and has gained an international reputation for research into unusual areas of psychology, including deception, humour, luck and the paranormal.

A passionate advocate for science, Professor Wiseman frequently appears on the media, gives talks and performances. He has written several books, including *The Luck Factor* - a bestselling book exploring the lives and minds of lucky people, and *Quirkology,* which explores the curious science of everyday life, including the psychology of lying, love and laughter.

Other titles in the series:

HOW TO
REMEMBER EVERYTHING

RICHARD WISEMAN

Quercus

First published in Great Britain in 2018 by

Quercus Editions Ltd
Carmelite House
50 Victoria Embankment
London EC4Y 0DZ

An Hachette UK company

A CIP catalogue record for this book is available
from the British Library

HB ISBN 978 1 78747 231 0

Jacket design by Setanta, www.setanta.es
Jacket illustration by David de las Heras
Illustrations by Amber Anderson
Author photo © Brian Fischbacher

10 9 8 7 6 5 4 3 2 1

Typeset by CC Book Production

Printed and bound in Great Britain by Clays Ltd, St Ives plc

To Whatshisname and Thingamajig

CONTENTS

Introduction

Welcome. Throughout this book you will be invited to participate in several interactive exercises. Do take part, because each one will reveal something important about your memory. Let's try one now. Please spend a few moments trying to remember these words –

bedroom, zebra, hat, chair, cup,
telephone, sandwich, socks

– and now turn to page 50.

– and now turn to page 50.

*

How did it go? It's unlikely that you remembered all eight words, although if you did, congratulations. Now for the second part of the exercise. Are you sitting comfortably? It's time to use your imagination and create a deeply strange story.

1

Imagine that your **bedroom** has a **zebra** in it. Assuming that you don't live next to a zoo with an astonishingly relaxed approach to captivity, that's going to be an unusual image. To make a strange situation even weirder, place a **hat** on the zebra. Maybe it's a top hat, a bowler hat, or a straw hat. It doesn't really matter. What's important is that the zebra is now wearing some kind of headgear.

Now let's pick up the pace and add some action. Suddenly, the zebra sees a **chair** and jumps over it. The leap is impressive, and so you award the zebra a **cup**. Seconds later, you pick up the **telephone** and order a celebratory meal. However, when the food arrives, you are somewhat disappointed to discover that it consists of a **sandwich** with **socks** inside it.

Tell yourself the story again and replay the scene in your mind each time. Now tell it to yourself one more time, but this time jot down all the words from the original list that you can remember (cover the top half of this page with a piece of paper first – no cheating!):

1 _____
2 _____
3 _____
4 _____
5 _____
6 _____
7 _____
8 _____

Now take a look at page 51. After replaying the story in their heads, most people are able to remember far more (and often all) of the words. Not only that, but they tend to remember the words in the right order!

My first mnemonic

A mnemonic is a tool that helps you to remember complicated facts and figures, and we are going to be discovering lots of my favourite mnemonics during our time together. I came across my very first mnemonic when I was 12 years old. A school friend said that she could teach me how to memorize this confusing 15-digit number in just ten seconds:

11221211122112

Sure enough, ten seconds later, I had the digits cemented in my mind. Even now, many years later, both the mnemonic and digits are still firmly lodged in my memory.

The secret will be revealed to you in this book ... eventually!

You have just used a simple mind trick to dramatically improve your memory. As we journey through the book we'll encounter lots more equally effective techniques. However, instead of learning how to remember words like 'zebra' and 'socks', these techniques will help you recall much more important information, including names and faces, birthdays and meetings, telephone numbers and shopping lists, and exam answers and pub trivia. Not only that, but you can use the techniques to impress your friends, to help keep your mind sharp, and even to change your life.

Along the way you'll discover lots of fascinating facts about your memory, find out how your brain remembers things (and forgets them), meet the man who could recall everything he ever saw (which made watching *Superman IV: The Quest For Peace* especially painful for him), and, of course, learn how to memorize the number for the mathematical term pi to nine decimal places.

I hope that you enjoy the journey and have an unforgettable time.

CHAPTER I

Johnny Mnemonic

It's time for another quick exercise. Imagine that you are an actor preparing for your first film. The film is called *An Alien Who Visits Earth, But Doesn't Know the Word For Lots of Everyday Objects*. As you might have guessed from the title, it's about a visiting and language-challenged alien who has come to our planet, Earth, but doesn't know the word for lots of everyday objects. You are playing the role of the alien and the opening scene takes place in a coffee shop. The camera finds you sitting at a table and a waiter, played by George Clooney, comes over to serve you. You are extremely thirsty. You look up at George and deliver your first line:

ALIEN: 'May I have a large container of coffee? Thank you!'

I would like you to rehearse the scene, and your line, in your imagination. And now... ACTION!

★

That was great, but could you do it again, and this time emphasize the word 'container'. And again... ACTION!

★

That was much better. Now repeat the scene a few more times in your head. Many thanks. We'll return to your film debut later on.

There are many millions of memories buried deep inside your brain. Most of the time, you are unaware of these memories, and wouldn't be able to recall them, no matter how hard you tried. But then, once in a while – BOOM! – one of these long-lost experiences suddenly pops into your mind. Maybe, when you walk into a small theatre, you suddenly remember your school staging *A Midsummer Night's Dream*, and everyone being horrified at Harold Findley's postmodern interpretation of Bottom. Or perhaps, when you are wandering in a park, you suddenly remember trying to impress Emily Wiltshire by climbing an unusually high tree, and how that ended up with you in hospital with a horrendous nosebleed. Or maybe, when you encounter the terrible smell of blocked drains, you remember how your grandparents used to visit every Sunday. Psychologists refer to these powerful signals as 'retrieval cues', and you can use them to remember important and useful information.

Let's start with perhaps the oldest and best-known retrieval cue. Imagine that you are back in a school science lesson. Your teacher writes the seven colours of the visible spectrum on the board, and asks you to make a note of them in your notebook. Then your teacher cleans the board, and asks you to close your book and remember the words. Within seconds, panic starts to set in. Try as you might, you just can't seem to remember the words. Finally, your teacher writes the magic phrase '**R**ichard **O**f **Y**ork **G**ave **B**attle **I**n **V**ain' on the board, and it all comes flooding back: '**R**ed, **O**range, **Y**ellow, **G**reen, **B**lue, **I**ndigo, and **V**iolet'. This type of mnemonic is known as an acrostic, and involves using the first letters from a group of words to help remember a phrase or list of words.

For instance, imagine that you want to remember the order of the planets orbiting the sun. It's tricky because there are nine planets (assuming you are in favour of Pluto as the most recently discovered planet), and you have to get them in the correct order. However, remember the sentence –

'**M**y **V**ery **E**ducated **M**other **J**ust **S**erved **U**s **N**ine **P**izzas'

– and you have made a seemingly complex problem super simple – **M**ercury, **V**enus, **E**arth, **M**ars, **J**upiter, **S**aturn, **U**ranus, **N**eptune, and **P**luto.

Creating the Perfect Password

You can use acrostics to create super-safe passwords. First, think of a memorable phrase, or song lyric, that's associated with the type of account that you are trying to protect. Next, take the first letter of each word in the phrase, or lyric, and use them to generate a unique and easily remembered password. For instance, if you wanted to create a password to your Apple Mac, you might think of the phrase '**An A**pple **A D**ay **K**eeps **T**he **D**octor **A**way', and so end up with the password '**AAADKTDA**'. *Voil*à, in seconds you have created a password that is easy to remember, but almost impossible to hack!

Acronyms and acrostics are just the tip of the mnemonic iceberg. There are also rhymes which can help you remember dates ('In fourteen-hundred-and-ninety-two, Columbus sailed the ocean blue'), and fun phrases (remember whether you should add or subtract an hour when the clocks change by using the phrase 'Spring forward, fall back' (as long as you don't forget that 'fall' means 'autumn').

Here are ten mnemonics that may get you out of a sticky situation at some point in your life:

8

1) If you ever get a chance to venture into the great American outdoors, avoid the dreaded poison ivy with the catchy phrase: 'Leaves of three, let it be'. Other plants may also have three leaves, but poison ivy often has one big leaf at the end of a stalk, and, below that, two smaller leaves on much shorter stalks.

2) If you find someone in a state of shock, remember: 'If the face is red, raise the head. If the face is pale, raise the tail.' A red face suggests that there's too much blood rushing to a person's head, whereas a pale face means that there isn't enough. Raising their head or feet assists blood flow and so helps to solve the problem.

3) Be alert to the signs of a heart attack by remembering the word '**PULSE**'.

> **P**ersistent chest pain
> **U**pset stomach (including nausea and vomiting)
> **L**ight-headedness
> **S**hortness of breath
> **E**xcessive sweating

4) To help find the right way of dealing with the pain of a bee or wasp sting, remember the '**AB:VW**' rule: **A**mmonia for a **B**ee sting, **V**inegar for a **W**asp.

5) If you have a sore throat and a runny nose, and you

want to know if you have a cold or the flu, look for the **'FACTS'**. The flu is associated with:

Fever
Aches
Chills
Tiredness
Sudden onset

6) When wiring a UK plug, the second letter of the colour of each wire tells you which side of the plug the wire goes: b**R**own to the **Right**, b**L**ue to the **Left**.

7) To remember which way to turn a screw or bolt, remember the simple phrase: **'Righty Tighty, Lefty Loosy'**.

8) Ensure that you set out the cutlery on a table correctly by remembering that the word KNIFE has the same number of letters as the word RIGHT, and the word FORK has the same number of letters as the word LEFT.

9) If you are at a formal meal and can't remember which is your bread plate and which is your drink, just form a 'b' and a 'd' with the thumb and first finger of each hand. Your bread plate is on the same side as the 'b' and your drink is on the same side as the 'd'.

10) Never again confuse your camels by remembering that the **D**romedary camel has one hump (like a **'D'**) whilst the **B**actrian has two (like a **'B'**). To be fair, this one probably

won't save your life. However, if you see a camel-based bank robbery, you'll be able to provide the police with a remarkably impressive eyewitness account.

And *these* ten mnemonics will help you to avoid common spelling and grammatical mistakes:

1) Avoid confusing the words 'stationery' (something that you use to write with) and 'stationary' (something that's not moving), by remembering that 'station**ER**y' is for lett**ER**s and p**E**ns, whereas 'station**A**ry' st**A**nds still.

2) If you struggle to remember the difference between the words 'desert' and 'dessert', just remind yourself that the 'de**S**ert' is **S**andy and that a 'de**SS**ert' is **S**ugary **S**weet.

3) Remember the difference between the words 'compliment' (saying something nice about someone) and 'complement' (when one thing goes with another) by using the phrase '**I** like to get compl**i**ments'.

4) Many people confuse the word 'principle' (an idea) with the word 'principal' (the head of a school or university). Solve the problem by remembering that a 'princi**pal**' is your **pal** and a 'princi**ple**' is a ru**le**.

5) To remember how many 'c's and 's's there are in the word 'necessary', remember that, like a shirt, the word has one **c**ollar and two **s**leeves.

11

6) Do you struggle to tell the difference between stalactites and stalagmites? If so, just remember that 'stala**c**tites' come from the **c**eiling and that 'stala**g**mites' come from the **g**round. Or if that's too tricky, you could just remind yourself that 'Tights ('**tites**') always fall down'.

7) When trying to spell the word 'rhythm', just remember that '**R**hythm **H**as **Y**our **T**wo **H**ips **M**oving'.

8) Spelling the word 'diarrhoea' is a piece of cake once you remember the phrase '**D**oesn't **I**t **A**lways **R**un **R**ather **H**orribly **O**ver **E**ach **A**nkle?'

9) If you struggle to spell the word 'separate', just remember the phrase: 'There's a **rat** in sepa**rate**'.

10) Finally, never again misspell the word 'mnemonic' by actually *remembering* the correct order of the letters. Only joking, in fact, it's '**M**y **N**anny **E**ats **M**ostly **O**ld **N**oodles **I**n **C**ans'.

Just before we end this section, let's return to your film debut. Once again, picture the scene in your mind. You are a thirsty alien from another world. You are in a coffee shop and George Clooney walks over. You look up and deliver your line. Can you remember it?

If not, here it is again: 'May I have a large container of coffee? Thank you!'

I hate to break it to you, but there is no film. I just needed a fun and effective way of cementing that line in your mind. Why? Because it allows you to impress your friends and win a bet. By the end of this book, you will be able to tell your friends that you are able to recite the numbers which mathematical term pi to nine decimal places. When they express their disbelief, you imagine that you are back in the café, and say your magic line. When your friends look perplexed, count the number of letters in each word of the line and you will end up with 3.141592653! (As long as you remember where to put the decimal point!)

CHAPTER 2

Think of a Number

Do you have difficulty remembering the Personal Identification Number (or 'PIN' for short) associated with your credit or debit card? Probably the easiest solution is for you to jot your PIN down on a piece of paper and send it to me, along with the sixteen-digit number on the front of the card. Just kidding. Almost no one would be silly enough to post their financial details to a complete stranger (although if you *are*, my address is at the back of the book). Yet millions of us engage in an equally risky activity everyday of our lives. Struggling to remember our PINs, and other equally important numbers, we keep written records of them in our wallets, purses, or diaries. If we are unfortunate enough to have these items stolen, we have essentially given our financial house keys to a criminal. However, the good news is that it's easy to learn some simple mind tricks that will allow you to store these important numbers in the most secure place possible – your memory.

Call Security

Here are two quick security tips:

- If you do keep a written note of your PIN in your wallet or purse, there's always the danger of a thief getting hold of it. To minimize the risk, disguise your PIN by, for instance, adding '1' to each of the digits (so that 7434 becomes 8545), or make it appear to be the extension to a fictitious telephone number.
- Once you have assigned the three-digit number on the back of your debit or credit card to memory, scribble over the digits on the card so that they can't be used should your card be stolen.

Most psychologists make a distinction between short-term and long-term memory. Your short-term memory contains the relatively small amount of information that you are aware of right now. In contrast, your long-term memory contains the vast amount of information and experiences that you have acquired during your lifetime.

You just used these two types of memory without thinking about it. In order to read the previous paragraph, you had to store each of the words in your short-term memory. However, even though you read the words just a few seconds ago, you will have already forgotten them. Instead, your brain will have extracted the general meaning of the paragraph, and stored it in your long-term memory.

Introducing the Hippocampus

Hidden away deep inside your head is a part of your brain called the hippocampus. This little packet of neurons is seahorse-shaped, and named after the Greek words for 'horse' (*hippos*) and 'sea monster' (*kampos*). Right now, it's busy working away, transferring information from your short-term memory to your long-term memory. It tends to deal with everyday memories (such as your memory for having breakfast this morning, or your memory of reading this book), rather than facts or figures.

During the onset of dementia, the hippocampus is one of the first bits of the brain to suffer, causing people to forget where they put their car keys, or if they locked their front door. However, if that does sound like you, there's no need to panic, because this type of forgetting is also associated with simply getting older and being busy.

Interestingly, if you are unlucky enough to damage your hippocampus, you will struggle to remember what happened yesterday, but will still be able to remember peoples' birthdays, and learn new physical skills (such as playing the piano, or juggling), thus showing that different types of memory depend on different parts of the brain.

When you encounter a number, your short-term memory stores each of the digits for a few moments. However, your brain then struggles to extract any meaning from the numbers, and so cannot store them in long-term memory. People often think that the only way to solve the problem involves endlessly repeating the digits until they become embedded in your brain through sheer brute force. This approach, employed by those teaching times tables the world over, is very hard work. However, help is at hand. Over the years, researchers have developed far easier ways of tricking your long-term memory into holding on to even the most meaningless of numbers.

Imagine turning over your new credit card and discovering that the three-digit number on the back is '070'. Remembering these numbers over the long haul will involve quite a bit of mental effort. Now imagine turning over your card and discovering that the number is '007'. You are far more likely to feel shaken or stirred – and remember it! Why? Because these numbers mean something to you and so are easy to store in your long-term memory.

Whenever you have the option of creating a number that you need to remember, choose something meaningful. Perhaps you can use your house number, or your children's birthdays, or the first few digits of pi. Make sure that you avoid using numbers that are easy for a criminal to figure out, such as the most commonly chosen sequences (currently 1234, 0000, 1111, 1212), or *your* birthday, or the last few digits of your telephone number.

If you don't have the option of creating a number, try to think of ways that an assigned number could become meaningful. For instance, let's imagine that you have to remember the number 1071, and that you are a football fan. You might remember that the famous footballer Pele wore shirt number 10, and played in his last international match in '71. Alternatively, visit one of the many websites that tell you whether it's possible to use the letters on telephones (just search for the words 'telephone' and 'spell') and ATM keypads to transform your number into a word. For instance, 3647 translates into DOGS and 4283 becomes GATE.

Telephone Numbers

At the start of the book you were asked to try to remember this list of words:

> bedroom, zebra, hat, chair, cup,
> telephone, sandwich, socks

Take a look at the words that you jotted down on page 51. My guess is that you will have been especially likely to remember only *some* of these words, namely:

bedroom, zebra, sandwich, socks

When people remember a list of letters, numbers or objects, they tend to recall the items at the beginning and end of the list. This is known as the 'primacy–recency' effect, and it can help you to remember telephone numbers.

If you try to remember this number

01378105733

the primacy–recency effect will kick in, and you will be especially likely to remember the digits towards the start (013) and end (733) of the number. However, if you break up the number into smaller groups like this

01378 105 733

you are likely to remember the start and end digits in each group, and so end up remembering many more numbers.

When you are trying to remember a telephone number, or are telling it to someone else, make it easy on the mind by breaking the number down into smaller groups of three or four digits.

Remembering Names

In the early 1970s, researchers from Bishop's University in Canada asked a small group of volunteers to look at thousands of photographs. Then, a few days later, the volunteers had to try to recognize as many photographs as possible. The researchers were amazed to discover that the volunteers remembered an astonishing 70 per cent of the total number. It seemed an unbelievable result, and, a few years ago, I decided to restage the study. I managed to persuade two brave volunteers to look at 10,000 photographs over the course of two days. The following day I tested them to discover how many of the images they could recognize. My results were consistent with the original study, and confirmed that our long-term memories can indeed store vast amounts of visual material. And the really good news is that you can use this quirk of long-term memory to help you remember important dates.

Why Two Codes Are Better Than One

Why are pictures better remembered than words or dates? It's a great question, and I am delighted that you asked. In the 1970s, psychologist Allan Paivio was studying how visual mnemonics boosted peoples' memories, and came up with his 'Dual Coding Theory' to explain what was going on.

The idea is surprisingly simple. Paivio proposed that your

mind stores information in two ways; verbally and visually (thus the 'Dual Code' bit). When you come across a picture, you unconsciously think of the words that describe the picture, and so generate two memories for it in your mind (one verbal and one visual). In contrast, when you look at a word, or a number, you don't usually think of a corresponding picture, and so end up with just the one memory (verbal). When it comes to remembering what you have seen, you have two memories for the picture, and one for the word, and so are more likely to recall the picture. However, use a mnemonic to turn the word into a picture, and, bingo, you have suddenly increased your chances of remembering the word.

Take a look at this illustration of digits and associated objects. Each digit and object resembles one another. For instance, a zero resembles a doughnut, and the digit 1 looks like a pencil, and so on. Take a few moments to familiarize yourself with the list and images.

Let's imagine that you want to use the list to remember the number 14. The 1 translates into a pencil and the 4 is a sailing boat. In a moment you'll be asked to conjure up an image involving these two items. However, before then, we need to disappear down a rabbit-hole.

Lewis Carol's *Alice in Wonderland* is full of wonderfully weird characters and happenings. Alice shrinks and grows. She meets a caterpillar smoking a water-pipe, a Cheshire cat who fades away leaving nothing but a floating grin, a Mad Hatter who is constantly partaking of afternoon tea, and the Queen of Hearts playing croquet with flamingos and hedge-hogs. When creating your own imagery, feel free to follow in Alice's footsteps, and create images that are strange and surreal. Make objects exceptionally large or small, use especially vivid colours, animate the objects in strange ways, tell fantastical stories, and incorporate smells, tastes, and sounds.

How might this apply to the pencil and the sailing boat? Well, maybe the pencil is standing in the boat and sailing across stormy waters. Maybe it's a giant pencil wearing a little captain's hat. Maybe the boat has a smiley face on the front of it. You get the idea. OK, create your image right now.

Now that we have cemented the number 14 in your mind, it's time to add an additional element. Here's a second list, one of associations linked to each month. (This is the list that I use; you might want to create your own.)

January	Cold
February	Love (Valentine's Day)
March	Marching
April	Joke (April Fools' Day)
May	The guitarist from Queen, Brian May
June	The actress, June Whitfield
July	Hot
August	Edinburgh Festival
September	Leaves
October	Halloween Pumpkin
November	Bonfire Night
December	Christmas Tree

Let's imagine that you are trying to remember the 14th March. The month of March is associated with the word 'marching', so maybe you could imagine the pencil marching back and forth in the sailing boat. Right-left, right-left, about turn, and so on. Cement that image into your mind. Finally, add a face to the pencil, and make it look like the famous physicist

Albert Einstein. Why? Because now you will always be able to remember Einstein's birthday – the 14th of March!

Let's try one more. How about the 8th of January? In my list, the 8 is an hourglass and January is associated with the word 'cold', so maybe you could imagine an hourglass shivering away in a fridge. Perhaps the hourglass is wearing a little embroidered white suit to keep itself warm. Now you have glued Elvis Presley's birthday in your mind too!

Once you get used to the idea, you'll be able to produce the images quickly and easily remember any date. On the downside, you'll have no excuse for missing the birthdays of your friends, partner, parents, or offspring ever again!

CHAPTER 3

Intermission

Let's take a quick break from the mnemonics, and engage in a different type of mind trick. Please carry out the following instructions:

- Think of any number between 1 and 9
- Multiply your number by 2
- Add 8 to your new number
- Divide your new number by 2
- Subtract your original number from your new number
- OK, now you have a number between 1 and 26...take that number and match it to its equivalent letter of the alphabet, with 1=A, 2=B, 3=C, 4=D, 5=E, 6=F, 7=G and so on
- Pick a country anywhere in the world that starts with that letter
- Now take the second letter of that country and think of an animal that begins with that letter
- Finally... think of the colour of that animal

Great, so now you have a randomly chosen animal, colour and country.

My guess is that your colour matches the colour of this book, and that your animal is the same as the animal on its front cover, and the country is the one printed at the bottom of the back cover!

Try it on your friends (avoiding those that love emus), and impress them with your magical skills.

I hope you enjoyed that. Now, let's get back to boosting your memory.

CHAPTER 4

Names and Faces

'I never forget a face, but in your case I'm willing
to make an exception'

— *Groucho Marx*

There's nothing I enjoy more than a good party. (Except,
perhaps, an excellent one.) However, I am not great at remembering the names and faces of the people I meet. A few years
ago researchers at Lancaster University carried out an experiment that revealed the root of the problem and suggested a
solution.

Let's imagine that you are a participant in my version of
the experiment. First of all, thanks for volunteering. In a
moment you are going to see a short paragraph describing
four people. Please try to remember as much as you can about
the people. Here we go.

First is Charlotte Fry. Charlotte is 58, a drama teacher,

and enjoys painting and playing the piano. Next we have Ben Baker. Ben is 28, works as an architect and spends his spare time hiking. Third is Sushmi Shyam. She is 25, studied philosophy at university and works in marketing. She is into mindful gardening and meditation. Finally, we have Ron Beard. Ron is 60, enjoys swimming and has trained as a master baker.

Wonderful. Now turn to page 51.

. ★

Welcome back. When the researchers carried out this experiment, they discovered something deeply strange, which was that the volunteers were far more likely to remember occupations and forget names (take a look at page 51 to discover whether this is also true for you). This was even the case when the volunteers were presented with exactly the same word – such as 'baker' – as either an occupation or a surname (did you find you forgot Ben Baker, but remembered that Ron Beard was a baker?).

The researchers were curious, and went in search of an explanation for this so-called 'Baker–baker paradox'. Eventually, they found out that it was all down to the relationship between long-term memory, meaning and imagery. In the previous chapter we discovered that your long-term memory finds it especially easy to store information that is either meaningful or visual. Names like Baker and Jones don't mean anything to you and aren't easy to visualize, and so are difficult to remember. In contrast, you know what bakers and accountants do for a living, and the words instantly conjure up images of a person with flour on their hands or a calculator on their desk.

On Labelling People

American President Franklin Roosevelt apparently employed a great mind trick to remember people's names and faces; whenever Roosevelt was introduced to someone he would imagine that person's name written across their forehead.

The technique works especially well if you visualize the name written in thick colourful permanent ink, and also secretly pretend to write the name with tiny movements of your first finger.

The good news is that these findings, combined with some of the techniques that we have learned in the previous chapters, can help you remember names and faces. Here are three tips for putting a name to a face:

1) *Listen Out For Their Name*
   When you meet someone for the first time, you're often focused on introducing yourself and thinking about what

you are going to say. As a result, you don't actually listen to their name. To overcome the problem, make a special effort to hear their name and, if possible, immediately repeat it back to them by saying something like, 'Oh, lovely to meet you, Richard'. And if you don't catch their name first time around, don't be embarrassed to ask them to repeat it.

2) *Use It Or Lose It*

Try to casually use the person's name as the conversation progresses, and think about ways of making it into a talking point. Maybe they share a first name with someone you know well ('Oh, that's my wife's name!') or perhaps they have an unusual surname and you can ask about its origins. If that feels odd, simply rehearse the name to yourself instead of saying it out loud. If possible, make a point of mentioning their name when the conversation comes to an end ('Richard, it was great meeting you, and I hope that we'll have the opportunity to chat again soon').

3) *Make A Good Mental Impression*

Try to represent the person's name in a visual image. Remember we are better at remembering things that are illustrated. As with all memory-boosting imagery, don't be afraid to journey down the rabbit hole and make it as strange and wild as possible. Here are a few handy hints and tips.

- Use any imagery which can obviously be associated with some names. For instance, Rose could be holding a giant rose, Scarlett could be covered in red paint, and Mike could be holding a microphone.

- If you know someone with the same name as the person that you have just met, imagine the two of them meeting. For example, maybe the person that you have just met is called Peter, and your three-year-old son is also called Peter. Imagine the two of them meeting, with hilarious consequences.

- If the person you have been introduced to has the same name as a celebrity, use that to create an image. For instance, you might imagine a person called Elizabeth holding a crown, or someone called Arnold as the 'Terminator'.

- If you are struggling to find an image, think about words that sound similar to their name. For example, 'Peter' sounds like the word 'eater', and so you could visualize him eating a sandwich. Also, try to break down longer names into smaller chunks. For instance, the image for Graham might involve a man with some 'grey ham'.

4) *Look For Something Distinctive About The Person's Face*
Do they have a mole, a large mouth, a delicate nose, thick eyebrows, or striking eyes? Try to link the image associated with their name to a distinctive aspect of their face. For instance, if Peter has a large mouth, you might imagine him eating his sandwich. Or, if Graham has bushy eyebrows, you might imagine some grey ham balanced precariously on them. Perhaps, if Elizabeth has small ears, you might imagine her crown as a huge ear-ring.

Let's give it a go. Here are four photographs showing the people from the Baker–baker experiment mentioned earlier on. What associations and images might you use to remember them? Try to find associations for each face, and then link them to the photographs.

Charlotte Fry   Ben Baker   Sushmi Shyam   Ron Beard

You will find out if this memory trick works for you … later on!

The Man Who Couldn't Forget

In April 1929, Solomon Shereshevsky appeared at Moscow's Academy of Communist Education, and asked to have his head examined. A young researcher named Alexander Luria presented Shereshevsky with several long lists of numbers, and his mysterious guest was able to remember everything. Intrigued, Luria continued studying Shereshevsky for decades, often asking him to remember complex scientific formulae, poems in foreign languages, and lists of letters in reverse order. Shereshevsky could memorize everything in a matter of minutes, and Luria was eventually forced to conclude that Shereshevsky's memory had almost no limits.

Shereshevsky's secret lay in his amazing, and highly unusual, imagination. He could effortlessly convert any number, or letter or word into a highly memorable vivid image, and would memorize lists of items by taking a mental stroll down a familiar street, imagining the items in various locations.

Unfortunately, the memories continued to haunt him. Shereshevsky's amazing memory was a double-edged sword. Unable to erase unwanted memories from his mind, Shereshevsky took to writing down everything that he wanted to forget on slips of paper, and then setting fire to the slips.

Shereshevsky performed as a professional mnemonist, but eventually turned to drink and died from alcoholism in 1958. Luria's book about his research, *The Mind of a Mnemonist*, has become a classic text, and provides unforgettable insight into the potential power of memory.

CHAPTER 5

Ten Top Tips

So far, we have discovered how to recall facts and figures, cement your PIN numbers and important dates like birthdays into your brain, and how to remember names and faces. Here are ten more scientifically supported tips to help boost your memory.

1) *Sleep On It*

Don't skimp on sleep. Research shows that when you are sound asleep your brain is busy discarding the information that you no longer need, and storing the facts and figures that you want to remember. If you have an important exam or interview, you might be tempted to stay up late and cram information into your brain. Fight the temptation. You are much better off getting an early night. Other work has shown that even a short nap during the day can boost your memory. If at all possible, follow in the footsteps of

President John F. Kennedy and Albert Einstein (born on the 14th March, as you know), and make napping part of your daily routine.

2) *Exercise Your Memory*

Researchers from the University of British Columbia assembled a group of volunteers and measured their memories. They then asked the volunteers to take a brisk, one-hour walk twice a week. Finally, they tested the volunteers' memories a second time and discovered that the energetic wanderings had significantly boosted the volunteers' memories. Resistance training, balance, and muscle-toning exercises all failed to produce the same positive effect. It seems that your memory only benefits when the exercise helps get extra oxygen to your brain, and so anything that gets your heart pumping is especially effective. If you aren't into walking, consider going for a swim, climbing up and down the stairs, playing tennis or squash, heading to the dance floor, or even doing some intense housework or gardening.

3) *Brains, Brussel Sprouts And Blueberries*

When it comes to memory, you are what you eat. Saturated and trans fats (found in red meat and butter) are bad for your brain and can disrupt your memory. In contrast, research conducted at the University of Pittsburgh has shown that a Mediterranean diet, rich in healthy unsaturated fats and Omega-3 fatty acids (think vegetables, fruit, olive oil, salmon, tuna, pumpkin seeds, brussel sprouts, and walnuts), is good for your brain and boosts your short-term memory. Additional research from the University of Exeter suggests that supplementing your diet with blueberries for 12 weeks also improves your short-term memory.

4) *Think Memory, Think Book*
Studies carried out at the University of Stavanger in Norway involved volunteers reading the same texts on either a modern computer screen or from an old fashioned piece of paper. Those who read the texts on the paper remembered far more about both fiction and non-fiction than those using a computer screen. The researchers believe that using your fingers to touch the paper may stimulate your brain, or that leafing through the pages helps you form a more memorable mental map of where you are in the text. Whatever the explanation, the message is clear: while screens might be fine for superficial reading, when you want to really remember what you read, reach for a book.

5) *Write It, Don't Type It*
In another study from the University of Stavanger, psychologists read out a list of words to volunteers and asked

them to note down each word immediately after they had heard it. Some of the volunteers typed the words into a computer using a standard keyboard, others typed them into a tablet using a virtual keyboard (that is, one presented on the tablet's screen), and a third group wrote the words by hand. The volunteers were then asked to remember the words. The volunteers who had written the words by hand recalled far more of the words. The psychologists believe that your brain is far more active when you are writing by hand, and so you are a lot more likely to be able to remember the information. In short, when you want to remember something – don't type it, write it.

6) *Be Quick On The Draw*
Researchers from the University of Waterloo in Canada presented people with a list of objects, such as 'car' and 'apple', and asked volunteers to either write the words down or draw a picture of the object. Later on, the volunteers were asked to remember as many of the words as possible. Those who had drawn the pictures easily outperformed those who had been busy writing down the words. The effect was far from trivial with those doing the drawing sometimes remembering twice as many as those who were only writing the names of the objects. The researchers also discovered that the quality of the drawings didn't matter –

suggesting that even the least artistic of us can benefit from this technique. When you want to remember something, be quick on the draw.

7) *Remember More By Seeing Less*

A study published in the journal *Legal and Criminological Psychology* examined whether witnesses to a crime might be better off shutting their eyes! Volunteers were asked to watch a video of a thief stealing stuff from a house and then to remember what they had seen. As they tried to recall the information, some of the volunteers were asked to keep their eyes open and others were asked to keep their eyes closed. The volunteers who closed their eyes remembered twice as many details as the volunteers who had kept their eyes open. The researchers believe that closing your eyes gets rid of distracting information in your immediate surroundings and so improves your memory of past events. Next time you want to remember something important, try closing your eyes.

8) *Chew It Over*

Psychologists from the University of Northumbria asked volunteers to take a 20-minute memory test whilst either chewing gum, mimicking chewing gum, or doing nothing at all. The results revealed that the gum-chewers scored

24% higher in tests of short-term memory and 34% higher in tests of long-term memory. The researchers are not quite sure why the effect works, and are currently chewing over the issue (sorry). Chewing gum increases your heart rate, and so it's possible that this results in more oxygen being delivered to your brain, which, in turn, boosts your memory. When you want to remember something, reach for the gum.

9) *White, No Sugar*

Researchers at Johns Hopkins University asked volunteers to study a series of images, and then take one of two pills. Half of the volunteers were given a 200-milligram caffeine tablet (roughly equivalent to a cup of strong coffee), while the others were given a placebo pill. The following day, the volunteers tried to recognize the images that they had previously seen, and those who had taken the caffeine outperformed those who'd received the placebo pills. However, as is often the case, timing is everything. Previous studies have shown that taking the caffeine *before* seeing the images has little effect. To boost your memory, reach for a mug of coffee, a cup of tea, or a can of soda *after* you have seen whatever it is you want to remember.

10) *Tie The Knot*

If you have to remember to do something, try tying a piece of string around your finger. As far as I know, there's no experimental evidence to support this technique, but I use it all the time and find it surprisingly effective.

Truth or Myth?

Take a look at each of these five statements about memory, and decide whether you think they are true or false:

1) People with amnesia can't recall their own names.
2) Hypnosis can help boost memory.
3) In a courtroom, the testimony from confident eyewitnesses should be seen as especially reliable.
4) Memory acts like a video recorder.
5) Some people have photographic memories.

Take a look at the answers on the page overleaf to see how many you got right!

Answers

1) People with amnesia can't recall their own name. **MYTH**. Actually, amnesiacs tend to remember who they are, and what happened in the past, but struggle to recall events that happened after their injury.

2) Hypnosis can help boost memory. **MYTH**. Placing people into a hypnotic state makes them highly suggestible, and so especially prone to describing details that are inaccurate.

3) In a courtroom, the testimony from confident eyewitnesses should be seen as especially reliable. **MYTH**. Research has shown that when it comes to eyewitnesses, there's no relationship between confidence and accuracy. Confident witnesses can be highly inaccurate, and people who appear unsure may in fact be accurate.

4) Memory acts like a video recorder. **MYTH**. Your memory *doesn't* record what is right in front of your eyes. Instead, it only stores certain information, and often distorts it.

5) Some people have photographic memories. **MYTH**. Some people claim to be able to look at a painting or photograph, and then 'see' a highly detailed image

of it in their head. However, tests of this so-called 'eidetic memory' have revealed that the resulting recall is not especially accurate. Similarly, memory champions don't have photographic memories either. Instead, they are highly skilled at using the mnemonics described in this book.

CHAPTER 6

Forget Me Not

We have now reached the end of our journey. Along the way we carried out lots of interactive exercises, and there is one final exercise to remind you of the various techniques that we have encountered. Ladies and Gentlemen, Boys and Girls, it's time for –

The 'How to Remember Everything'
Really Big Memory Test

The test involves four items.

1) At the very start, I presented you with eight words, and asked you to imagine a fun scene involving animals leaping all over the place. Replay the story in your mind and see how many of the words can you remember.

2) We then discovered how acronyms, acrostics, rhymes, and phrases can help you remember important facts and figures. I asked to you play the role of a thirsty actor in a film about aliens and everyday objects, and to remember a single sentence which unlocks the numbers which express the mathematical term pi to nine decimal places. You are back in the cafe. You are thirsty. Up walks George Clooney. What's you line?

My line is: _____

3) We then moved onto ways of remembering your PIN, telephone numbers, and birthdates. It was all about making the numbers meaningful, and using vivid imagery. At the end of the section I asked you to form two images that

would help you remember the birthdays of Albert Einstein and Elvis Presley. Can you remember the birthdays?

Albert Einstein's birthday is: _____

Elvis Presley's birthday is: _____

4) Finally, we moved on to names and faces, and discovered how listening, repetition and association can help you put a name to a face. I introduced you to four fictitious friends of mine. Here are their photographs again:

Can you remember their names?

The name of the first person is: _____
The name of the second person is _____
The name of the third person is: _____
The name of the fourth person is: _____

Answers

To save you the trouble of going back through the book, here are the answers.

1) Give yourself a point for each one that you remembered out of: bedroom, zebra, hat, chair, cup, telephone, sandwich, and socks. (Maximum score: eight points.)
2) 'May I have a large container of coffee? Thank you!' Award yourself a point for each correct word. (Maximum score: ten points).
3) Albert Einstein's birthday is on the 14th of March, and Elvis Presley's birthday falls on the 8th of January. Once again, one point for each correct answer (a maximum of two points).
4) Their names are Charlotte Fry, Ben Baker, Sushmi Shyam and Ron Beard. Award yourself one point for each correct first name or surname (Maximum score: eight points).

Add up your score and let's see how you fared.

0–7: You might want to go back to the beginning of the book and start ... again.

8–13:   Not bad, but there's still some room for improvement.

14–19:   That's better. Nice to see some of the information cemented in your memory.

20–28:   Congratulations! You win the **S**hereshevsky **M**emory **A**ward for **R**ecollection and **T**hinking and you are (easily remembered using the acronym) officially **SMART**.

And so there we have it. I hope that you have enjoyed our whirlwind tour through the innermost workings of your mind, and that you can use the various techniques to develop a super-powered memory.

Oh, talking of which, I nearly forgot something. At the very start of the book I described how, as a twelve-year-old boy, I encountered my very first mnemonic. As you might remember, a school friend taught me how to memorize this confusing 15-digit number in just ten seconds:

11221211122112

It's still my favourite mnemonic, and has stuck in my mind over the years. Do want to discover the secret? All you need to do is just remember this fun rhyme:

11 was a racehorse
22 was 12
11 1 1 race
22 11 2!

Have fun sharing it with others, and I hope that you will always remind you of our time together!

Sorry, I have a terrible memory for numbers. My mistake, please go to page 51.

Thanks for playing along. Please jot down the words that you can remember here.

_____

_____

_____

Thanks. And now return to page 1 ...

★

Please jot down whatever you can remember about the four people.

Person 1: _____

Person 2: _____

Person 3: _____

Person 4: _____

Many thanks. And now return to page 28 . . .

Acknowledgements

This book wouldn't have happened without my wonderful agent Patrick Walsh, and fab editors Jon Butler and Katy Follain. Also, special thanks to David Britland, David Berglas, and Mike Page for their expertise and inspiration. And finally, as ever, this book wouldn't have happened without the wonderful support of my partner, Caroline... Oh, what's her surname? Begins with 'W'. No, it's gone. Anyway, a huge thanks to her, too.